BIRDS

WILL COME
TO YOU

OTHER BOOKS
by the
AUTHOR

- FRISKY, TRY AGAIN!

- COME TO THE CIRCUS

- A FOX IN THE HOUSE

- MR. STRIPES THE GOPHER

- WHEN WINTER COMES

BIRDS

WILL COME
TO YOU

by
**CHARLES
PHILIP
FOX**

The photographs were taken by the
author whose children, Barbara and Peter
are shown in many of the pictures.

**REILLY & LEE CO.
CHICAGO, U.S.A.
1963**

ACKNOWLEDGMENT

The beautiful paintings of the cardinal and blue jay used on the jacket are the work of Owen J. Gromme of Milwaukee. The engravings for these paintings, as well as the color separations, were made by the Mueller Engraving Co. of Milwaukee and loaned for use in this book.

Grateful acknowledgment is made to Mr. Gromme and to the Mueller Engraving Co.

DEDICATION

*This book is dedicated to all of my many
friends who find so much pleasure
in birds, especially*
CHARLEY AND MARY NELSON

A CHUNK of suet spiked to the top of a post makes a perfect winter feeder for many birds.

Seen here is the handsome Blue Jay intent on procuring a meal. The chunk of suet could be tied to the trunk of a tree, or fastened to the windowsill.

Your pleasure comes in watching the birds; so locate feeders where they can be seen from your home.

TABLE OF CONTENTS

	Page No.
INTRODUCTION	9
WINTER	
ATTRACTING BIRDS IN WINTER	11
PHOTOGRAPHS OF FEEDERS	12 thru 31
WHAT TO FEED	32
KEYS TO SUCCESS IN WINTER FEEDING	32
SUMMER	
ATTRACTING BIRDS IN SUMMER	33
PHOTOGRAPHS OF BIRD HOUSES	33 thru 55
KEYS TO SUCCESS IN BUILDING BIRD HOUSES	62
PLANTING TO ATTRACT BIRDS	69
KEYS TO SUCCESS IN PLANTING	69
PHOTOGRAPHS OF BIRDS' NESTS AND EGGS	70 thru 86

INTRODUCTION

THIS FINE BOOK, so easy to read and understand, will serve as a worthwhile guide to those of us who wish to become better acquainted with birds.

A very successful approach to the subject in simple language has been maintained throughout the book. The excellent photographs and diagrams are so presented and explained that with little effort and ingenuity and a few basic tools, our feathered friends can be induced to feed and nest in our dooryard, and to tarry with us as long as food is provided, or the urge to migrate moves them out in spring or fall.

Mr. Fox, in an understandable manner, shows the way for any one of us from nine to ninety to create a whole new world of interest in their own yard and garden.

OWEN J. GROMME,
Curator
Dept. of Higher Zoology
Milwaukee Public Museum

BIRDS WILL COME TO YOU
IN WINTER

Does it surprise you to know that many beautiful birds do not fly south in winter?

Even if you live where snow and ice take over from October to March, you will still find birds nearby. They will afford you even greater pleasure in winter than in summer—for winter is the time when it is so easy to coax the beautiful and lively birds to come to you!

Before the snow falls, birds are able to find berries, grains, fruits, and kernels on the ground. They find seeds which in the fall were dropped by trees, bushes, grasses, and plants. In the country they search farmer's fields for kernels of grain, and in the city they discover food in woodlots, fence rows, hedges, and plantings in the parks.

But when winter drops the temperature and covers your community with ice and sleet, it locks up all such food, and the birds go hungry. The sun may melt the ice sheath in a day or two and unlock the food supply temporarily. But when snow again covers the ground, fences, trees, and such deserted birdhouses as the one in our picture, the birds are in great peril. The weather change which to us means only a beautiful snowfall is a great disaster for the birds. They have a hard struggle, as they turn to the few withered crab apples still clinging to the trees or pine cones defying the wind high in the evergreens. Even road-killed animals are a source of food in such a time. Everything and anything will do during the birds' great winter fight for survival.

When birds are hungry they quickly lose their habits of shyness toward man. Birds do not really fear you—they just usually do not need you to exist and are able to take care of themselves. In winter, however, the birds will gladly accept your hospitality if you put out food for them. In exchange you will have the pleasure of seeing these lively and beautiful creatures close at hand, and nothing so livens a drab winter day as these eager visitors flying about near your windows. Depending upon where you live, anywhere between five and twenty-five varieties of birds will respond to your hospitality. And it is so easy—so inexpensive—and so much fun!

A few strokes of the shovel or broom, a handful of breadcrumbs, and you have made, quickly and easily, a simple winter feeding ground. The English sparrows, shown here, are like a gang of boys at recess. There is constant action as they fuss, fight, and hop around while eating.

Birds are creatures of habit; therefore, once you start to feed them and get them in the habit of depending on you, it is only fair to them that you keep it up. If you feed only occasionally, the birds will go to more reliable sources for food.

Here is a suggestion for helping winter birds. Instead of throwing away your Christmas tree, make it into an inexpensive and attractive feeding station. Push the trunk into a snow bank near a window. Then melt three or four pounds of suet and mix in chopped nuts, raisins, and grain of any kind. When you pour the mixture over the branches the cold chills the suet so that it clings to the needles, holding the feed for the birds. Many of them enjoy the suet, too.

Another good idea is to pour the melted suet with its chopped nuts and grains into dixie cups or cardboard cheese containers. After the suet hardens, the cup can be cut away and the suet chunk can be tied to a branch of the Christmas tree. For that matter, it can be tied to the branch of any tree and attract birds within view of a window in your home.

This picture shows a very easy feeding tray to build under any first floor window. The advantage of this tray is the ease with which it can be swept clean of snow. Even little boys can replenish the food supply. The edge around the top of the tray keeps the wind from blowing the feed onto the ground, and soon chickadees, juncos, and nuthatches will be flashing on and off to enjoy a meal.

The photographs in this book are meant to give you ideas. The drawings are meant to give you only general dimensions. Feel free to alter any of these ideas to fit your budget, the tools you have, or the scrap boards you can find. For example, the legs on this tray need not be the cleanly planed boards shown—they could just as easily, and far more cheaply, have been made of branches cut from any tree.

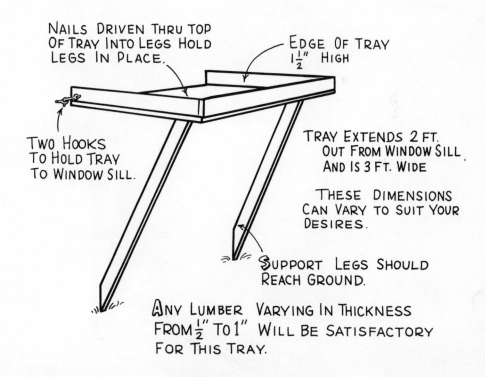

NAILS DRIVEN THRU TOP OF TRAY INTO LEGS HOLD LEGS IN PLACE.

EDGE OF TRAY 1½" HIGH

TWO HOOKS TO HOLD TRAY TO WINDOW SILL.

TRAY EXTENDS 2 FT. OUT FROM WINDOW SILL AND IS 3 FT. WIDE

THESE DIMENSIONS CAN VARY TO SUIT YOUR DESIRES.

SUPPORT LEGS SHOULD REACH GROUND.

ANY LUMBER VARYING IN THICKNESS FROM ½" TO 1" WILL BE SATISFACTORY FOR THIS TRAY.

Here is a tray for a second floor window. Because the windows swing outward, this tray had to be mounted far enough away to let the windows clear it when they are opened. The roof on this tray is not necessary, but it helps to keep off rain and snow. The open sides give the birds a sense of freedom, and they will quickly feel at home. Supports for the roof can be made from bits of lumber or branches cut the right length. If you decide on branches, do not trim off the twigs. They become fine perches.

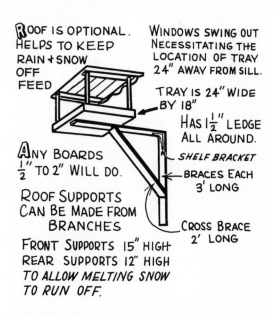

ROOF IS OPTIONAL. HELPS TO KEEP RAIN + SNOW OFF FEED

WINDOWS SWING OUT NECESSITATING THE LOCATION OF TRAY 24" AWAY FROM SILL.

TRAY IS 24" WIDE BY 18"

HAS $1\frac{1}{2}$" LEDGE ALL AROUND.

SHELF BRACKET

ANY BOARDS $\frac{1}{2}$" TO 2" WILL DO.

ROOF SUPPORTS CAN BE MADE FROM BRANCHES

BRACES EACH 3' LONG

CROSS BRACE 2' LONG

FRONT SUPPORTS 15" HIGH REAR SUPPORTS 12" HIGH *TO ALLOW MELTING SNOW TO RUN OFF.*

The little girl looking out at the chickadees has learned that if she stands perfectly still the birds will approach within a few inches of her nose. This tray has a small hopper to hold feed. There is also a small perching branch on one corner.

Here are photographs of various visitors seen from inside the house.

Photograph 1 is a beautiful cardinal. She has a heavy and strong beak with which she can crack open seeds.

Photograph 2 shows evening grosbeaks enjoying sunflower seeds. These birds are handsomely colored in yellow and black with white wing tips. They are also quite tame.

A blue jay is seen in photograph 3. When you feed birds in winter it is easy to get good pictures. They will come into camera range and pose prettily. Good photographs of birds at a window feeder can be taken with the simplest camera.

The feed hopper in photograph 4 is one easily made with only a hammer and saw. The sketch is merely a suggestion and the hopper can be larger or smaller. But there is one space which must always be the same—the one inch slot for the grain. If it is larger, the grain will pour out too rapidly. If it is smaller, it may become clogged, particularly after a snow. The feeder suggested here will hold about a quart of grain.

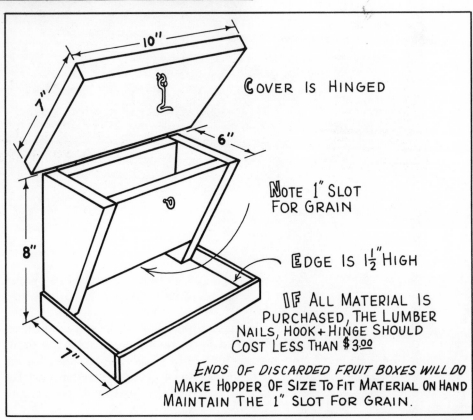

10"

7"

COVER IS HINGED

6"

NOTE 1" SLOT FOR GRAIN

EDGE IS 1½" HIGH

8"

IF ALL MATERIAL IS PURCHASED, THE LUMBER NAILS, HOOK + HINGE SHOULD COST LESS THAN $3.00

7"

ENDS OF DISCARDED FRUIT BOXES WILL DO MAKE HOPPER OF SIZE TO FIT MATERIAL ON HAND MAINTAIN THE 1" SLOT FOR GRAIN.

Attractive feeders can be made from cocoanuts by simply sawing "V" shaped pieces from one side of the shell. Not only do the birds enjoy the cocoanut meat, but the inside is a perfect place to put gobs of peanut butter, grain, breadcrumbs, or other food.

Two ways are shown to fasten cocoanuts so that the birds can get to them. The nut on the right has a screw turned through the branch up into the shell. The other nut is hanging from a screw-eye turned into the top. If a feeder tray is not available, these nuts can be fastened to branches of a tree. The two birds are black-capped chickadees, some of the liveliest of the winter visitors.

In photograph 1 a hairy woodpecker is busily pounding off a piece of suet. Birds like this suet feeder because it is easy for them to cling to it as they eat. Also, because of its construction, the snow and ice never completely cover it. This feeder can be made in less than an hour and without any cost except for the hook, which could be exchanged for a piece of cord tied to a branch, if desired.

The sticks can be cut from any bush or tree and pushed into drilled holes in the wooden top. If the sticks are larger in diameter than the hole, the size can be whittled down with a jack-knife. The chunks of suet should be inserted before the sticks are tied together at the bottom.

The white-breasted nuthatch is a trim-looking bird who loves suet. Always alert, he is shown in photograph 2 as he pauses for a quick look around before he resumes pecking at the chunk of suet on the feeder platform.

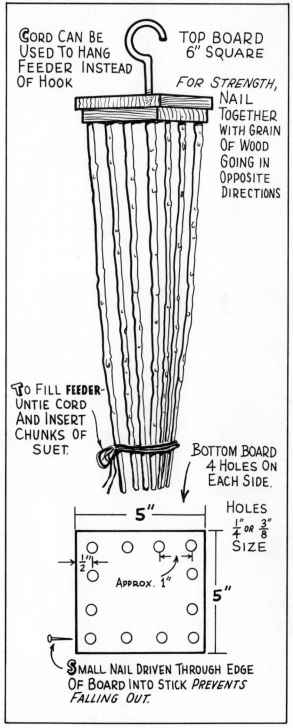

CORD CAN BE USED TO HANG FEEDER INSTEAD OF HOOK

TOP BOARD 6" SQUARE

FOR STRENGTH, NAIL TOGETHER WITH GRAIN OF WOOD GOING IN OPPOSITE DIRECTIONS

TO FILL FEEDER—UNTIE CORD AND INSERT CHUNKS OF SUET.

BOTTOM BOARD 4 HOLES ON EACH SIDE.

HOLES $\frac{1}{4}$" OR $\frac{3}{8}$" SIZE

5"

$\frac{1}{2}$"

APPROX. 1"

5"

SMALL NAIL DRIVEN THROUGH EDGE OF BOARD INTO STICK *PREVENTS FALLING OUT.*

23

Here is one of the quickest and easiest ways to attract birds. A piece of suet tied in a netted bag and hung from the limb of a tree makes a feeder which needs no tools. This little red-breasted nuthatch specially likes the netted bag, for her feet hold to it easily, even upside-down.

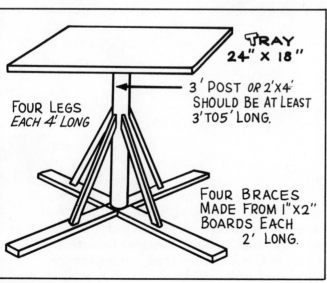

TRAY
24" X 18"

3' POST OR 2'X4'
SHOULD BE AT LEAST
3' TO 5' LONG.

FOUR LEGS
EACH 4' LONG

FOUR BRACES
MADE FROM 1"X2"
BOARDS EACH
2' LONG.

This tray is nailed to the top of a stump and has a feed hopper like the one on page 20. The platform is 24 by 18 inches with a one-inch edge which keeps the feed from blowing away. The tray could easily be fastened to a post as shown in the sketch, and put wherever it can be seen from a window. Blue jays are eating the grain.

With deep snow covering their normal food, this flock of twelve beautiful hen pheasants came within ten feet of the house to feast on corn. Ever alert, they would go running or flying off at the slightest movement but soon would hurry back to get more corn. To make the pheasants feel more secure and protected, branches were laid on the ground. On the right is a feeder which held about two bushels of ear corn. Made from chicken wire with a two-inch mesh, it was three feet high and 18 inches wide. Two iron rods driven into the ground kept it from tipping, but strong sticks would do as well as

the rods. The pheasants were able to get at the corn, and snow could not cover the ears. The advantage of the easy-to-make feeder shown on the left is that it too keeps the corn up off the damp ground, while also making it easy for the birds to get.

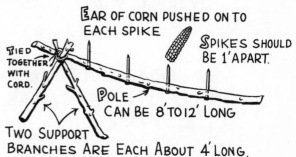

EAR OF CORN PUSHED ON TO EACH SPIKE

SPIKES SHOULD BE 1' APART.

TIED TOGETHER WITH CORD.

POLE CAN BE 8' TO 12' LONG

TWO SUPPORT BRANCHES ARE EACH ABOUT 4' LONG.

HOPPER IS 12" WIDE AT TOP
TAPERING DOWN TO A $1\frac{1}{2}$" SLOT
THRU WHICH GRAIN FALLS TO
FEEDER TRAY

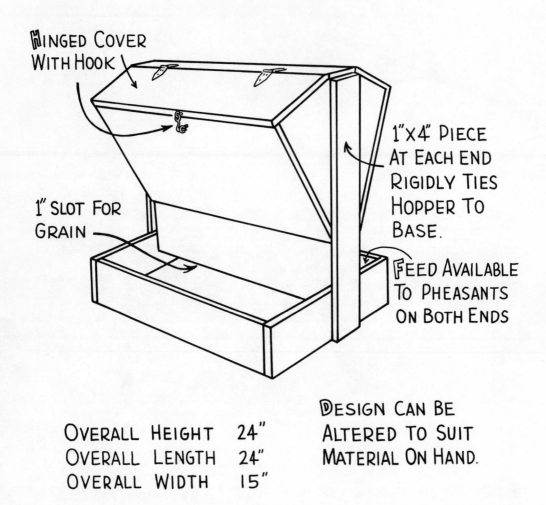

HINGED COVER
WITH HOOK

1" SLOT FOR
GRAIN

1"x4" PIECE
AT EACH END
RIGIDLY TIES
HOPPER TO
BASE.

FEED AVAILABLE
TO PHEASANTS
ON BOTH ENDS

OVERALL HEIGHT   24"
OVERALL LENGTH   24"
OVERALL WIDTH   15"

DESIGN CAN BE
ALTERED TO SUIT
MATERIAL ON HAND.

MATERIAL CAN BE $\frac{1}{2}$" OR $\frac{3}{4}$" OR $\frac{7}{8}$"
WHICHEVER IS AVAILABLE.

In the above picture two gloriously colored rooster pheasants are quietly sneaking through the brush pile to get grain from the feed hopper. Pheasants will come much more readily if brush is piled nearby. This hopper holds nearly a bushel of grain which falls into the tray as the birds eat.

The hopper in the picture is only a suggested design. It can be made to suit whatever wood and tools you have on hand. But again it is important to be sure the grain slot is exactly one inch wide. You do not have to be a good carpenter or even paint your feeder if you don't want to. Birds don't care how the feeder looks, they just want to be sure of getting the grain. But a painted feeder will of course last longer and can be used through more winters.

In the picture to the right, ears of corn have been tossed into a briar patch of blackberries. Pheasants prefer to feed in cover. Ears of corn tossed under evergreen trees, or bushes, give them the same feeling of protection.

Squirrels are pretty little animals, but they can be a great nuisance. When a squirrel hops onto a feeding tray, the birds have to wait until the squirrel is stuffed with food before they dare approach. The feeder to the left was on the windowsill of a stucco house, which the squirrel climbed with ease.

The picture above shows three ways which make it easy for squirrels to invade a feeding tray. First, the support post is wood which the squirrels can climb. Second, the tray was near a tree from which they can easily jump. Third, it was also near a building, making it easy for them to leap down from a porch or from the roof. Squirrels will always steal bird food if they can, but there is one sure method of stopping them—cover the post with sheet-metal and place the feeder away from trees and buildings.

KEYS TO SUCCESS FOR
WINTER FEEDING

1. Start to feed early in the fall, and do it constantly all winter.
2. Feed the right kind of food, as listed below:

WHAT TO FEED

1. Bread crumbs
2. Suet.
3. Common chicken scratch feed
4. Cracked corn
5. Wheat
6. Millet
7. Hemp
8. Chopped peanuts (or any other nuts)
9. Apples and raisins
10. Weed seeds of any kind
11. Screenings obtained from grain elevators
12. Ground up dog biscuits (high in protein)
13. Canned dog food (remove from can, place in netted onion bag and tie in tree, as the suet is tied in the picture on page 24)
14. Sunflower seed (this is expensive, but it is the food most birds like best)

BIRDS WILL COME TO YOU
IN SUMMER

Here is the same birdhouse as the one in the snow scene which was the picture on page 10. But it is spring now, and birds are looking eagerly for places to live and bring up their families. There are two basic ways to attract interesting bird visitors in summer—one is to build bird houses they will use; the other is to plant trees, bushes, and ground cover in a way which makes them feel at home.

More than twenty different birds commonly use man-made boxes, or platforms for their nests. Our friend in the picture happens to be a bluebird. He is looking for a suitable home, but he doesn't care a bit about fancy carpentry or paint. You can forget neatness, sandpaper, paint, or varnish, as far as he is concerned. But he does want to feel protected by being near a tree or spreading bush, and he likes low plants or long grass nearby for his hunting grounds. In return for your hospitality he will not only flash colorfully past your windows and sing his beautiful songs, but all summer long he will be eating the insects who would otherwise be spoiling your garden.

Birds will come to live in houses you have built and put up for them.

A robin will build on any ledge or platform large enough to hold its nest. Here a piece of board was tacked under an eave next to a window. The robins built their nest, laid blue eggs, and brought up their family—all where the children inside the house could watch every day from the window. It was a fascinating sight. Robins build a nest of coarse grasses which they line with a wall of mud. This, in turn, is lined with fine grasses. The birds are good engineers, and it is wonderful to watch them. Then comes the excitement of seeing the young birds come out of their eggs, eat, grow, and finally learn to fly—all right under your eyes.

When watching birds who are so near, you have to remember that too much motion from inside the house may frighten them away. When you come to the window, always walk slowly. The mother robin, although she knows that a watcher is there, will sit quietly on the nest as long as no one moves suddenly to worry her.

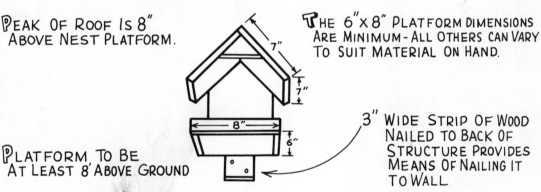

PEAK OF ROOF IS 8"
ABOVE NEST PLATFORM.

THE 6"x 8" PLATFORM DIMENSIONS
ARE MINIMUM - ALL OTHERS CAN VARY
TO SUIT MATERIAL ON HAND.

7"

7"

8"

6"

3" WIDE STRIP OF WOOD
NAILED TO BACK OF
STRUCTURE PROVIDES
MEANS OF NAILING IT
TO WALL

PLATFORM TO BE
AT LEAST 8' ABOVE GROUND

Here is another kind of robin-nesting platform. Because it was nailed to the side of a garage, a protecting roof was added. This was done to keep the hot sun off the birds, and also to give them a feeling of being safely hidden. If the robins were nesting in a tree, the leaves would give them the same feeling.

Robin nesting sites do not need sides. Robins enjoy an open platform, which should be about six inches square. It should also be at least eight feet above the ground. Scrap ends of boards, a few nails, a saw and hammer are all you need to make this attractive house.

Most of the bird houses in this book are so easy to build that with a little help almost any child can make one, but this does not mean the birds like these houses any the less. A simple, unpainted bird house is often much prettier than any amount of bright paint could make it. The sun and rain will soon give it a soft silvery color, and it will fit naturally into the landscape.

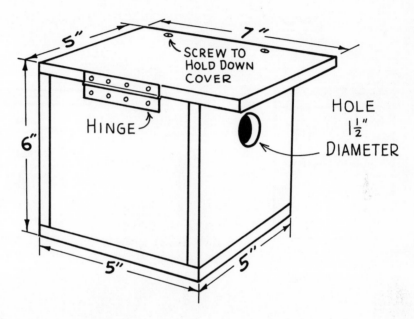

5"

7"

SCREW TO
HOLD DOWN
COVER

HINGE

HOLE
1½"
DIAMETER

6"

5"

5"

HINGED COVER NOT ESSENTIAL.
IT DOES MAKE IT EASY TO CLEAN HOUSE.

These houses will suit several kinds of birds. Bluebirds, tree swallows, crested flycatchers, chickadees, and even wrens, will enjoy them. A little branch nailed to the front of a house makes any bird feel more at home.

Birds have an inherent desire to nest in the spring. They also have an inherent desire to build a certain kind of nest in a certain kind of location. Being creatures of habit makes it easy to attract them to your yard. You need only to build a house that simulates what they are instinctively looking for.

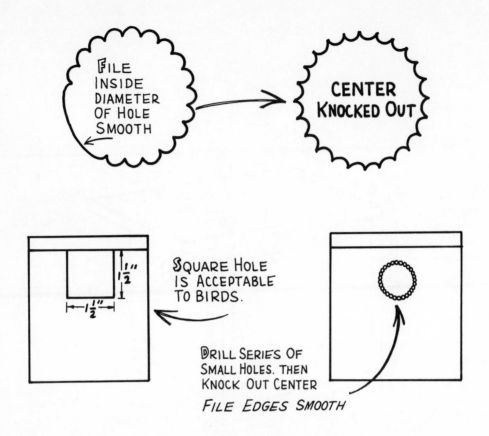

FILE INSIDE DIAMETER OF HOLE SMOOTH

CENTER KNOCKED OUT

SQUARE HOLE IS ACCEPTABLE TO BIRDS.

DRILL SERIES OF SMALL HOLES. THEN KNOCK OUT CENTER

FILE EDGES SMOOTH

The hole in the birdhouse in this diagram can be bored with an extension bit, but if you don't have a bit of that kind, you can make the hole as shown above. Mark out the hole in pencil, then drill smaller holes along the pencil line as close together as possible. When the circle of small holes is ready, knock out the center and file the rough edges smooth. A square hole will do, but does not look as neat as a round hole.

In the picture on the right a tree swallow is seen using one of these houses. Two of the four young birds in the house already hear the flutter of incoming wings and are reaching out to be fed. One of the most beautiful birds, the tree swallow has a shimmering blue and green back which glints in the sun. A graceful flyer, the swallow swoops about snatching insects out of the air. Its grass nest is generally lined with soft white feathers, in which it lays from four to seven white eggs. This house was fastened to a grape arbor about five feet above the ground.

Birds will live in houses bigger than they really need. That is why so many different birds will use this kind of house. If they can fit through the hole, and if the inside is large enough for them to build a nest, they will like this box.

43

The pearl gray breast of the crested flycatcher is a lovely contrast to the olive green feathers of its wings and back. The nest it built in this house to hold the three to six brown-streaked cream-colored eggs is made from twigs and rootlets lined with soft grasses. Here the hungry young await the dinner of mayflies which their mother holds in her beak.

This birdhouse was designed for flickers. The floor is seven by seven inches and the two-and-one-half-inch diameter hole is about fourteen inches above the floor. The house can be nailed to a post approximately eight feet from the ground, or it can be nailed to a tree at this height. Flickers are fond of ants and are frequently seen on the lawn devouring them by the score. Coaxing a flicker family to live nearby is a great help in keeping grass and walks free from anthills.

Here is a group of wren houses fresh from the workshop of the hobbyist. Such houses are delightfully easy to build, and no birds more readily accept the offer of a man-made dwelling than the wren. Their cheery warbling song and bustling energy make them desirable birds to have nearby.

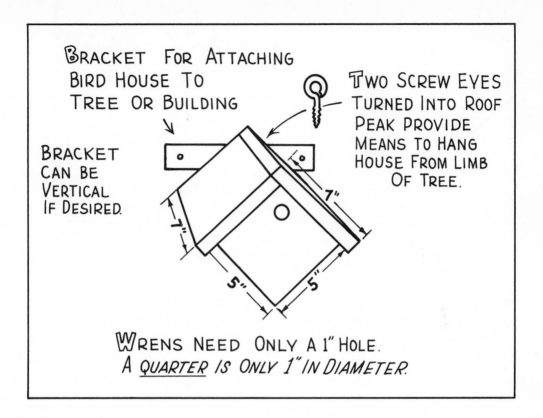

BRACKET FOR ATTACHING
BIRD HOUSE TO
TREE OR BUILDING

TWO SCREW EYES
TURNED INTO ROOF
PEAK PROVIDE
MEANS TO HANG
HOUSE FROM LIMB
OF TREE.

BRACKET
CAN BE
VERTICAL
IF DESIRED.

7"

7"

5"

5"

WRENS NEED ONLY A 1" HOLE.
A QUARTER IS ONLY 1" IN DIAMETER.

Different ways of hanging wren houses are shown in the picture to the left. The two boxes in the background have boards across the back for easy nailing to a building or the limb of a tree. One of the boxes has screw eyes turned into the roof by which it can be hung. No wren minds having his house swing in the breeze. The twig perches are optional. The birds use and enjoy them, but do not need them. They are merely an inexpensive way to make the houses more attractive. Necessary to build these houses are only the simplest tools, plus the basic information given in the chart on page 63.

The roofs on most of the houses overhang about an inch and a half to shield the hole from rain and sun.

Many birds like nesting in hollow trees or deserted woodpecker holes. The hollow logs here were found in a farmer's woodpile, but fallen trees with hollow centers can be seen in almost any woodlot, if you look for them. Simply cutting the logs into sections makes ideal birdhouses. If you don't think you can saw through the logs yourself, any lumberyard can do it for you in a jiffy for a very small cost. The larger hollow logs can be cut into fifteen-inch lengths to make homes for flickers. The smaller logs can be cut into eight-inch lengths for bluebirds, tree swallows, or wrens. Different ways of making holes are shown in the photographs. Boards nailed to top and bottom serve as roof and floor.

In this family scene a father wren brings caterpillers to his mate, who for a moment has left the eggs she is incubating on the nest inside. The wren's nest is made of twigs, lined with grasses and feathers, and it fills the entire cavity of the house. In it the wren lays six to eight minutely speckled eggs. This birdhouse is the same as the one in the center of the picture on page 48, where the roofs had been put on and the houses were waiting to be hung outdoors.

Both the flicker house at the top of this page and the bluebird house at the bottom were made from the hollow log sections shown on page 48. The flicker house was put about ten feet above the ground, while the bluebird house was placed on the grape arbor.

Sometimes one can find a fallen tree with a woodpecker hole in it. A section of such a tree makes a perfect bird house. The log can either be set into a hole in the ground or tied to an upright post. Either method makes a natural birdhouse which needs no material or tools to build.

This flicker is enjoying his log house and feeding ants to his hungry brood through the old woodpecker hole.

Here are other logs serving as natural bird houses, and giving the setting a pleasantly rustic look. The evergreens provide wonderful cover and attract birds to enjoy the feeding ground and to move in and establish families. For birds this is an ideal place to live. The taller log has two holes. The first year a flicker used the lower hole, while a chickadee raised a lively brood in the one above.

Purple martins are among the few birds who live in colonies, and it is great fun to watch life in their busy "apartment houses." Building apartments for martins looks harder than it actually is. A martin house is merely larger than other birds' houses and has to be put up higher in the air, and it is well worth the bit of extra trouble, for martins are lovely in song and flight and will be with you from early spring until August. A good place for a martin house is near water, but this is not essential. The most important rule is never to place it in a grove, or even within fifty feet of trees, for martins need open spaces in which to swoop and fly. A martin house can be as plain as you wish, or ornamented to suit your imagination. It can be any shape and contain any number of apartments, but in addition to location there are a few other basic rules. Each apartment must be at least six inches square. The hole should be at least 2½ inches in diameter and be not more than one inch above the floor. The house should then be placed on a pole at least 15 feet off the ground.

If you follow these simple rules, martins will flock to you in great numbers and soon your house will be a busy colony. Each martin nest is a simple affair of twigs, grass, and perhaps a few leaves, so the martin house seldom needs cleaning between seasons. You will, however, have to clean it if sparrows or starlings have nested there. A martin scorns any house which has been filled with rubbish by starlings and sparrows. In fact, these nuisance birds will actually drive martins away, as will squirrels if they are too inquisitive. A piece of sheet metal about three feet wide nailed around the post will keep squirrels from climbing to the house.

The perching arrangement shown on the pole is used by the martins. It adds interest, but it is not necessary. A couple of ½ inch dowels, six or eight feet long, nailed to the pole will do just as well as iron rods shown in photo.

BILL OF MATERIAL
for
MARTIN HOUSE
on Page 54

Item No.	Description	Size	No. Req'd.
1	Roof	18″ x 36″	2
2	Top Ends	11″ x 24″—1 Hole	2
3	Perch	2″ x 12″	2
4	Floor	30″ x 32″	2
5	Bottom Ends	6″ x 24″—3 Holes	2
6	Shelf Brackets	12″	4
7	Post	4″ x 4″ x 15′	1
8	Top Sides	6″ x 25½″—3 Holes	2
9	Bottom Sides	6″ x 25½″—1 Hole	2
10	Partitions	6″ x 8″	12
11	Long Partitions	6″ x 22½″	4
12	Ceiling Panel	22″ x 24½″	1
13	Steel Bracket	4″ x 4″	24

* Nail or screw together as desired.

* All material used is standard ¾″ lumber

MARTIN HOUSE

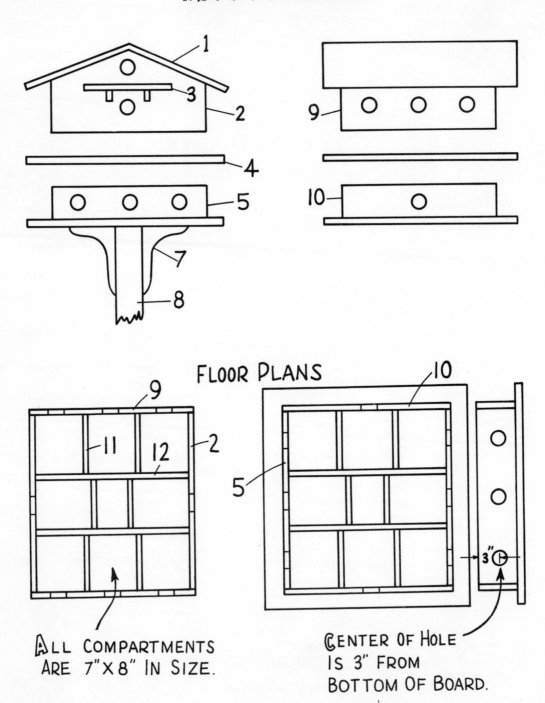

FLOOR PLANS

ALL COMPARTMENTS
ARE 7"x8" IN SIZE.

CENTER OF HOLE
IS 3" FROM
BOTTOM OF BOARD.

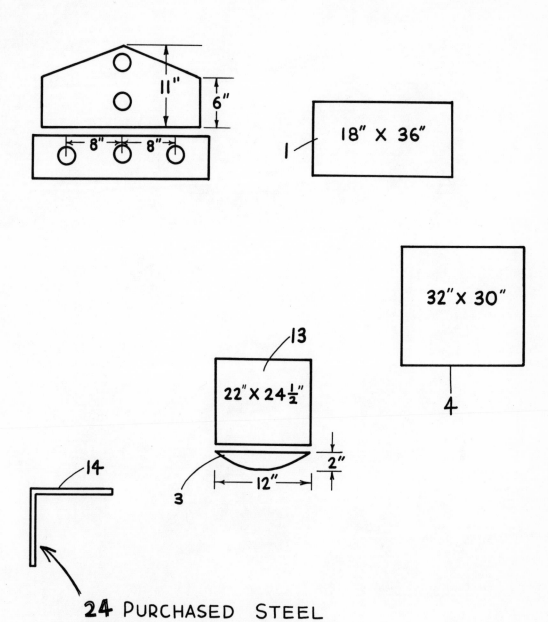

11"

6"

8" 8"

1 18" X 36"

32" X 30"

4

13

22" X 24½"

2"

12"

3

14

24 PURCHASED STEEL
BRACKETS 4"x4" HOLD
TOP AND BOTTOM SECTION
TO FLOORS

To the left, a little screech owl, hardly bigger than a flicker, perches on a stump. At dusk, the owl, ear tufts erect and round eyes wide open, may be seen ready to fly away on silent wings in search of food. Almost the entire diet of this bird is insects or mice, young rats, moles or other rodents. He is a great help to any healthy flower or vegetable garden and farmers are always pleased to see him near their fields, for he gets rid of many pests. During the day, the owl may roost in a hole in a rotted out stump, where he peeks out safely at the world until finally at dusk he flies off to go hunting. His tremulous, melancholy call is a delight to hear in the quiet night.

KEYS TO SUCCESS FOR BUILDING AND LOCATING BIRD HOUSES

1. Correct minimum hole size.
2. Correct minimum inside dimensions.
3. Correct height off the ground.
4. Correct location (the bird's desire; not yours).
5. No holes or cracks at bottom of nesting box. Birds will leave a drafty house.
6. Do *not* put nesting materials in any bird house except for wood ducks, who like two or three inches of sawdust or shavings. (See wood duck specifications for house size and location on following page.)
7. Rainproof (no holes or cracks in roof).
8. A hinged side or cover is helpful when the bird house is cleaned after a brood has left the nest, but such cleaning is not absolutely necessary.

On the next page is a chart giving complete information as to sizes of nesting spaces, height above ground, and other specific rules for building bird houses. Some fifty kinds of birds use boxes or platforms. The twenty birds listed are those who are most easily attracted and most commonly nest in man-made shelters.

BIRD HOUSE
CHART

BIRD	Floor of Cavity Inches	Depth of Cavity Inches	Entrance Above Floor Inches	Diameter of Entrance Inches	Height Above Ground Feet
Barn Swallow	Any simple ledge or platform				8–12
Bluebirds	5 x 5	8	6	1½	5–10
Carolina Wren	4 x 4	6–8	1–6	1	6–10
Chickadees	4 x 4	8–10	6–8	1⅛	6–15
Crested Flycatcher	6 x 6	8–10	6–8	2	8–20
Downey Woodpecker	4 x 4	8–10	6–8	1¼	6–20
Flicker	7 x 7	16–18	14–16	2½	6–20
Hairy Woodpecker	6 x 6	12–15	9–12	1½	12–20
House Finch	6 x 6	6	Front Side Open		8–12
House Wren	4 x 4	6–8	1-6	1	6–10
Nuthatch	4 x 4	8–10	6–8	1¼	12–20
Phoebe	6 x 6	All sides open			8–12
Purple Martin	6 x 6	6	1	2½	15–20
Red Head Woodpecker	6 x 6	12–15	9–12	2	12–20
Robin	6 x 8	All sides open			6–15
Saw-Whet Owl	6 x 6	10–12	8–10	2½	12–20
Screech Owl	8 x 8	12–15	9–12	3	10–30
Sparrow Hawk	8 x 8	12–15	9–12	3	10–30
Tree Swallow	5 x 5	6	1–5	1½	10–15
Wood Duck	10 x 10	22–24	18	5	10–25

Before ending our section on birds who will come to you in summer, a word or two should be said about birds who do not live in bird houses but who may be attracted to nest or feed near you. One of the most interesting is the barn swallow, who is easy to please and attract. A barn swallow likes to plaster his mud pellet nest to the joists of a garage, shed, or barn. He may even use a breezeway or porch of a house. One or two nails, or a one-inch square strip of wood on a joist helps to coax swallows to move in. The doors of a building intended for a swallow's nest must be kept open at all times during the nesting season.

In the picture above, the male barn swallow wonders how long his nest will hold his growing family. His mate hangs on the side of the nest, where she has just fed her hungry young.

These nests are wonderful examples of construction when one considers the size of the birds who build them. When the brood of the barn swallow finally moves out of the nest and huddles together on a perch, one knows that in a day they will be off and flying. One marvels at their ease and grace in flight as they skim over the fields in pursuit of insects.

Another bird easily attracted in summer is the hummingbird. These color-ful and charming little creatures are like winged jewels and will come readily to feeders holding honey-water, or sugar-water. As in the picture above, the simplest glass vial pleases them. Hung on a stick in a flower bed or garden, this man-made nectar draws the beautiful little birds as if it came from the sweetest of flowers. The ruby-throated hummingbird seen above is but one of eighteen kinds of hummingbirds found in the United States.

With wings beating at high speed, the hummingbird hovers over the cup to drink sugar-water. Any small glass bottle, jar, or test tube will do, and it may help catch the bird's eye if it is painted bright red or orange to imitate a flower in the garden. The National Audubon Society, 1130 Fifth Avenue, New York 28, N.Y. has hummingbird nectar feeders for sale.

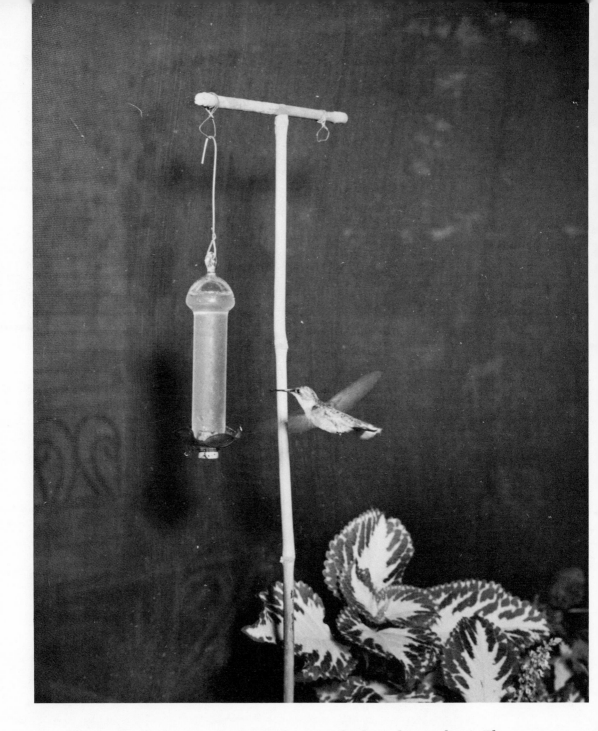

Another kind of nectar feeder for hummingbirds is shown above. These tiny little creatures flash brilliantly in the sun as they hover near the cups to drink. Then they dart away so quickly that it is hard to see them. And, remarkably, they can fly backwards too.

PLANTING
TO ATTRACT BIRDS

Birds will nest in many different kinds of places, which makes it easy to attract them no matter what your surroundings may be. You may find nests in tall grass, shrubs, bushes, grape arbors, small saplings, big trees, or even on an unused gravel driveway. Careful planning and planting will attract birds just as well as an expensive landscaping project.

A good place to start is along fence lines, or in a corner. What to plant will depend upon where you live and the type of soil you have. You can determine, by your own likes or dislikes, a happy medium of planting between a highly manicured garden or a wild entanglement of uncut grass, vines, and bushes. You will find birds coming to whatever you have to offer. After you know the basic rules, you can develop your own backyard sanctuary.

Remember this—when birds are nesting they are seeking a hiding place. They want a feeling of security where they cannot be seen by their natural enemies. Bushes and trees serve a double purpose: they are nesting sites and they also provide food. Plants bearing seeds or fruits which will ripen and then cling to the branches should be kept in mind as sources of food for winter birds.

Your program can be planned according to the size of your land and the fullness of your pocketbook. To help you decide exactly what to plant in your area, write your Conservation Department at the State Capitol and ask for pamphlets available on bushes, trees, and other planting suitable for your soil and geographical location.

KEYS TO SUCCESS IN PLANTING

1. Plant in clumps.
2. Plant thickets.
3. Plant ground cover.
4. Plant along fence lines.
5. Plant vines alongside brush piles.
6. Plant a variety of trees and bushes.
7. Do not cut grass, or manicure the lawn near the plantings.

BIRD NESTS
IN THE YARD

Birds reward you generously for your interest in them. They bring their glorious variety of melodious song and magnificent array of brilliant plumage in all its many shades and tints. Then, too, they bring a highly utilitarian appetite for insects of all kinds, who might be eating your garden—if the birds were not already eating *them*!

For a short few weeks in the spring the birds also bring to you nature's miraculous phenomenon of nesting, laying eggs, and rearing young. Birds who nest in houses can be seen best when busily bringing food to their young, but birds who nest in bushes on the ground or in trees give you an opportunity to watch the mysterious hatching of their delicate eggs.

Nests vary in construction from the barn swallow's complicated mud pellet engineering to the simplicity of the kildeer, who just shuffles aside a few stones on a disused driveway and calls the result home. Nevertheless, all nests are located and built with the idea of screening the occupants from natural enemies. The kildeer's eggs look quite like stones, and that is why she puts them on old driveways. Most birds, however, depend on bushes or trees to hide their nests, and that is why birds in great numbers will come to you if you have made an effort to plant bushes or trees to give them proper cover.

The incubation period ranges from twelve to fourteen days for the song birds; up to three to four weeks for pheasants and ducks. This is a touchy period, for if the mother birds is frightened from her nest during this time she is apt not to come back to her eggs at all.

If a nest is being watched near your house, never touch the eggs or the nest. This is a sure way to make the bird desert her brood before it is hatched.

The photographs on the next few pages show a few of the birds who can be coaxed to nest near your house, whether your lot is fifty feet or many acres.

In the tangle of long grass along a fence a shy song sparrow found a secluded spot. To the little boy, the eggs looked like gems to be picked up and cherished, but he had been taught only to look and never touch. This little sparrow hatched her eggs and reared her young just a few yards from the boy's house, and he had the joy of watching the baby birds grow up and fly away. Any boy or girl has much more fun watching birds live and grow than could possibly be had by stealing the eggs or nest. In any case, it is now a Federal offense punishable by law to damage, destroy, or collect eggs or nests of song birds.

This picture shows how much the kildeer's eggs look like the stones among which they are laid. A kildeer nests on a stony field or in an abandoned drive-way, where it can be in the open and see everything that is going on. When the kildeer leaves the nest, the mottled chocolate coloring of the eggs blends perfectly with the stones and almost hides them from view.

Framed in lovely blossoms of bridal wreath, this catbird is busy feeding its young. This inconspicuous bird, with its plumage of slate gray and black, has one of the most musical of songs, and sings almost constantly. Only when frightened does it utter the cat-like meow for which it is named. Its eggs are a lovely greenish blue, as rich as the finest Oriental enamel. The catbird is attracted to dense thickets or clumps of bushes, and like all song birds, has a voracious appetite for the insects which attack flowers. A hungry song bird is a garden's best friend.

The beautiful goldfinch (often called "wild canary" because of the male's brilliant yellow and black plumage) builds its delicate nest in a shrub or a bush, a small evergreen tree or a sapling apple tree, as in the photograph above. The nest is made of grass, strips of bark, and perhaps moss before being lined with thistledown to form a soft hollow for the pale, bluish-white eggs.

The bronzed grackle, with its shiny purplish-black feathers and piercing yellow eyes has no song, but is an asset to any garden because of its appetite for destructive insects. This grackle nest is in a red cedar tree only a few feet from the house. The pale blue eggs are marked with cinnamon and black scrawls. Sometimes these birds will nest in colonies in a clump of evergreens.

Nervous because someone is peeking into her home, the mother robin above scolded and made a great fuss from her perch on the porch, while her nest in a nearby tree (see picture to the right) intrigued a little boy. It was tucked into a dense spruce, and the beautiful shiny blue eggs were nestled in a soft grass lining within a casing made of mud. The robins had shaped it into a perfect cup in which they could raise their family.

The song of the robin in early morning, or late afternoon, is pleasant to the ear, and the sight of the robin feeding her speckle-breasted young is equally a delight to the eye. After about two weeks of incubating, the eggs hatch, and the father and mother begin the almost incessant job of feeding the young, who eat always their own weight in worms and insects every day.

If, by chance, you live near a marshy area, an entire new group of birds will serenade you. The marsh will harbor the Virginia rail, coot, red-winged blackbirds, swamp sparrow, and an endless list of other birds, including the American bittern, which lays its pale olive colored eggs on a platform of grasses on the ground, or in grassy meadows along ponds and creeks or among reeds as in the photograph above. The bittern makes a strange booming, pump-like sound which once heard will never be forgotten.

A brush pile in a corner will often attract birds, such as the nesting pheasant above. These birds like a tangle of brush as much as they do open fields. Where there are lots of homes and people, a brush pile makes a pheasant feel safe. The hen lays ten to twenty olive-colored eggs of different shades. As soon as her chicks hatch, she will leave the nest and take her brood into woodlots or fields of tall grass where she finds safety and food.

Another bird who likes a brush pile is the mallard. If you live near water, you may be able to coax her to nest in a pile of cleverly placed tree-cuttings. In the picture she is well hidden by her protective color, as she quietly sits on her "clutch" of greenish buff colored eggs.

An even dozen eggs are in the mallard's nest. Mallards, like all birds, want a quiet and secure place. The thrill of seeing the duck with her fluffy brood trailing after her as she leaves the nest is ample reward for your trouble in making a brush pile available for her.

Any small woodlot near a suburb or housing development is an inviting
place for woodpeckers, kingbirds, chickadees, whip-poor-wills, scarlet tan-
agers, and many others. The tall trees also lure hawks, such as this red-tailed
hawk who has built his nest seventy feet above the ground. Each year the
same pair of hawks will re-use this nest, perhaps adding a few more sticks
to its bulky structure and relining it with grass or bark. Invaluable to the
community, because of their insatiable appetite for rats and mice and other
rodents, these hawks are a beautiful and thrilling sight as they soar in
restless circles high in the sky.